The Art of Impossible

Serendipity Upon the Road of I'm Possible

Richard Schultz

OutBack Insides Publishing

The author has represented and warranted full ownership and/or legal right to publish all the materials in this book.

The Art of Impossible
Serendipity Upon the Road of I'm Possible
All Rights Reserved.
Copyright © 2013 Richard Schultz

Cover Photo © 2013 JupiterImages Corporation. All rights reserved used with permission.

This book may not be reproduced, transmitted, or stored in whole or in part by any means, including graphic, electronic, or mechanical without the express written consent of the publisher except in the case of brief quotations embodied in critical articles and reviews.

OutBack Insides Publishing

ISBN: 978-0-578-11779-9

PRINTED IN THE UNITED STATES OF AMERICA

My greatest joys and my greatest challenges have been through my personal friendships....I am always up for more joy and challenge. I am also open to causal hellos and instant goodbyes. If your desire to communicate falls somewhere within these parameters, I can be reached at rschultz010@yahoo.com I've got a great feeling we are all full of surprises.

By all means feel free to share excerpts with others as this book was written for inspirational purposes.

Dedicated to my German Shepard, Marley.

Never have I been witness to the Bar of Happiness set so high.

Inspired by Debra Darr, Josh, Ry, and Lil Jess.

Rocket, don't roll it!

Contents

The Abyss Quietly Beckons 1

Bungee Jumping Without the Cord 5

We Are Not the Skins We're In 15

Finding Friends in Fear and Folly 23

Reality Remembers Its Riddles and Rhymes 43

Working the Streets of Soul Smarts 57

Becoming What Is Because We Already Are 87

A Kiss or Frog Legs in the Soup? 129

The Abyss Quietly Beckons

How can in some moments we know and become, while in others only hope to happen?

How can the life within us, that remains a constant, be so fleeting?

How can one's heart bend, for one, to be only broken, by another?

How can we rush so fast to arrive in a place we only want to leave in a hurry?

Why does our wind blow, to be blown by each other, to blow another away?

Why do we shake our earth to swallow that which we rest so securely upon?

How can blood within the saints be spilled to become the marrow of those who sin?

How can a heart give until it is only taken away?

Do we actualize within our existence or are we actualized without, because there is no within?

Do our bodies travel freely only to be imprisoned by our spirit?

Do we separate our hearts, segregate them, silence them?

Are our stomachs fed and that which longs for meal left starving?

Do we let go, to be let down, from being done?

Is heaven a place we reach to take another unto, only to share the hell when we have arrived?

Do we walk away when come hither begs?

Bungee Jumping Without the Cord

John Lennon wrote the lyric:

"Life is what happens to you while you're busy making other plans."

It was just me caught in the sea of humanity, immersed in my separate reality, with no hand to hold unto. Strained, my participation, anxious anticipation, making other plans when life's crashing wall of water happened down on me. Nature has no preference, you know, life is a vast scale. An easy mark, she plunged me wholly through the gaping holes of my archaic consciousness.

It's hard to explain, maybe it was just a ridiculously late mid-life crisis because I wasn't sure emotionally and spiritually what was happening to me.

Here I was in my 50's, haunted by the naive innocence and intelligence of my youth. In all reality, my world, emotionally, physically and spiritually, was utterly disintegrating.

Free falling without a parachute is a certainty in life. This is why we are born with wings to soar.

I felt as though, I had been transported in a time capsule, asking and answering so many emotionally charged situations confronted in my younger days. Shrouded I was, within the mystery of,

Serendipity:

Exceptional fortune coming out of unexpected circumstances. A knack for making fortuitous discoveries, entirely looking in a different direction.

A combination of events which are not individually beneficial, but occurring together produce a bountiful and unexpected outcome.

In other words, digging for worms and discovering gold. Folks in Texas know, oil from a water well.

Unmistakably, the entirety of my life has been a serendipitous event. Life itself is an experience of potent unbridled potentiality. Life itself is a self sustaining event. How can life be blamed for anything?

This quaint bit of prose was a coming home for me, a confirmation of my own consciousness: The primal instincts of human being are not necessarily, in the greater interest of being human.

I needed to bring crystal clarity to my own senses. This bit of a read was written as if I were sleep walking. It genuinely is just the endeavored consciousness of my 20's. Little did I know then, the challenges it would all encompass as I grew older.

My teenage years were spent in the early 70's, rock-n-roll, life's exhilaration, instinctual co-mingling, passionate and introspective ways. A lot of my generation grew up like that.

We all had our different style; we all played our own tune. It's the same thing over again with the youth, different symphony, the beat never goes away.

Countless numbers in my generation, legions of youth today, are maturing, instilled with a high sense of idealism.

Life is a thin line of integrating our conscious will and actions, allowing external natural cause, where without, we micromanage circumstances.

Where within, we allow ourselves the rock to roll.

We as a species are no different in regard to so many other species in our quests within the domain of Mother Earth. Nature is constantly leveling the playing field. Natural law supersedes human imposition, regulating controlling aspects of religious and man-made law.

Life is the consummate equalizer. The ultimate bulldozer that turns us all under and we become weeds along the roadside or flower into our own individualism.

These musings were purposely written so a fifth grader can understand them. They can easily be read in one sitting.

Nothing you will read here is rocket science. It's honestly just getting back to the basics. That has been my intent all along.

I have discovered most fifth graders have a far higher bar of unconditional consciousness than most adults.

I have had my own joyful and humbling long-term experiences with the youth. I have learned from them there is a time for adults to get out of the way.

My bottom line regarding the youth is to live dual realities.

If you look at the progression of the human species, each generation succeeds the one prior, in releasing constrictive ideology and dominant behavior.

So in all reality, I observe and listen intently, I always ask myself:

Who's teaching who?

Remarkably with ease, the writings began encompassing the relationship I now experience within myself. I began reflecting on the emotional challenges of my own life.

The challenges my friends of all ages are facing within themselves and those they love.

I reflected on how personal growth is enhanced, when transmuting friends to lovers and back again to friends.

This transformative experience has always intrigued me, and equally troubling, it is such a glaring hole in many long term and unhappy ending relationships.

If you have ever been friends, seriously fantastic friends, when entering into a long-term relationship, it is worth every aspiration possible to regain that friendship. Regardless of the heartache, sorrow, and dissolution both parties share in the aftermath of a crumbling, committed, relationship.

There is something irresistibly miraculous regarding unabashed honesty. There is something so remarkable shared in unconditional hugs. There is something so awe-inspiring between two people recognizing, we are people, and because of this we have our imperfections and shortcomings.

There is something so inspiring, where love and communication are always present, yet spans of time go by, where there is neither a voice heard, or a written word sent.

I have my anchors.

I have soul smarts. I have my heroes.

I wasn't about to sink.

Early on I came to the conclusion many years ago: There are girls, there are women, and there are angels that inhabit the feminine embodiment.

Although I am many miles away and many years apart, the inspiration of those I love, the mere remembrance of them, is a coming home for me.

⁂

As quickly as this creative flame had been ignited, is as assuredly, the flame extinguished.

I knew from the beginning the message must be evoked by another consciousness and not determined by my will.

I knew the moment, I separated the one word, Impossible, into the two words, I'm Possible.

I had to let go.

I had to let me go.

I gave the key away to let somebody else open the door. The key of consciousness.

I challenged the part of nature within me that had challenged me.

My own magic to assure magic is within me.

My point here, I simply ask you to continue reading, see the pictures within the pictures of your own life.

The inner pictures.

The portrait of your soul.

Peer squarely into the life that transpires within you while you're busy making other plans.

Look for yourself.

In so many ways, life's puzzle you are completing, is the same one I am completing, the picture is one of:

Serendipity. Impossible? Give it up. You, like me,

Serendipity Upon the Road of I'm Possible.

We Are Not the Skins We're In

It appears the moments are waning, and the last of many interactions are closing in, as does the sun set, when the moon is restless to rule the night.

So a thousand miles will part us, yet miles are minnows in the belly of a whale, and many times the connection of a soul is stronger a half a world apart.

I want to tell you, straight up, you have your trust and heart vested in a place where even the angels fly boldly, yet wings of flight, fall mercilessly when stuttered by procrastination.

I want you to know, there is no running from hearts that love you.

In a moment, I will tell you what the Sun is, sun tan lines, and the deepest seeds that rest, dormant, to give way to the longing of the expressions of life.

The body is such a deceptive animation. We rely on it, and others judge it to be where we exist. There is sentimentality expressed, family gatherings, life's travels.

I learned a long time ago, the body, like the spiritual and emotional parts of us, needs to be cleansed, blown away and stripped down. We thrive on new beginnings.

We are all constantly living and dying or constantly dying and dying.

Folks get sad when our bodies eventually disappear.

Kids are devastated; hearses enjoy a full tank of gas. Less and less grass find a new blade to sprout come spring, because another set of footprints, bringing flowers that will die, tread upon their space.

It wasn't my idea to create all this. I either put up or give in.

※

If it were my life, I would have created me. I would have made myself by me.

It is life, and life expresses itself through me.

My choice is to be a bubble upon life's waters or sea beneath.

※

Keep in mind, we did not create ourselves, we were created by a greater.

It is not hard to realize with that understanding that our possibilities are far more than what we can perceive.

Fear and lack of consciousness are committed deterrents to actualizing potential.

It is easy to become afraid if we think we are simply just who we are, but we are not, we are greater.

If we created ourselves, we would simply be who we are.

Allowing momentarily, a desire to know how we got here, creates an alignment with the source of our origination.

Now is an eternal moment. At this moment try consciously to step out of this moment. Step away and remove yourself from this moment.

Try harder.

Try again and remove yourself from this moment.

Tie yourself to a team of horses, strap on to the Space Shuttle, you can't make it happen!

OK.

We tried and where did we go? Where are we now?

The eternity of now.

How is it that our minds attempt to exist in a yesterday that has passed, a tomorrow that never comes, when there is no earthly way possibly stepping away from the existence of now?

Is it just me, or do we try insistently to do this?

Sitting here at this moment, we can discover the potentiality of the entirety of our existence.

The existence of now.

Stepping outside of oneself and looking inside of oneself, is a startling way to discover who we are.

Physically looking into a mirror we actually see a tiny segment of what we are comprised of.

The moment we walk away from a mirror we take remarkably little of what we see with us.

We are connected to what we see, but we are not existent within it.

A physical mirror offers hardly a clue as to where we actually exist. The reason it is difficult for our inner eye to perceive is because our outer eye is always looking away.

We all sleep within the same bodies that we utilize while we are awake. Yet how can that be, when there is no consciousness of our bodies while we are sleeping?

Within deep sleep, there is awareness, there is consciousness, yet where is our body?

Where are we, and who are we, if we are not there?

Every night we are someplace, where we are not, or are we?

Say again?

We exist within our own multiple being.

We exist separated within the wholeness of ourselves.

Our minds and bodies tag along and try their best to keep up with who we actually are, so do our emotions. Our spirit will continuously dissolve and transmute our thoughts and emotions, leaving what we were once thinking, and feeling far behind.

How is it we retain our individuality within a sea of humanity, constantly pitting our will against each other, though intertwining our emotions at the deepest levels?

We cannot and do not fully live, one without the other.

Integrative wholeness will always use the will of resistance, actively blended within its opposite, the emotions of passivity.

Life is manifested by our will but truly embraced by our emotions. A conscious will infused with emotion, gleans ingredients of its own choosing, creating a life of reality, surrounded by a countenance of its own making.

This is where the heart knows no fear.

This is where the soul is rewarded by its own valor.

Soulful living is an art. It is a pursuit.

It is a craft.

For some it must be taught, for others it happens naturally. As a rule, it is the most optimum life course one can take. It is the most optimum because it is our own.

It is not a matter of being good or evil as one may judge through the eyes of religion or immorality.

It is not an opinion from another.

It is a matter of finding our own inner compass and embarking on its personal direction.

This compass can be found by courageously removing debris.

Our soul is constantly prohibited from its own expression by our emotions and our perception of mental judgment.

Achieving soul awareness is extraordinarily similar to what a sculptor does with rock or marble.

Continuously remove from the mass. Chisel again and again.

Never add. Only take away.

Finding Friends in Fear and Folly

Life starts out a bit unpleasant because of our utter helplessness and subjected dependency. Life is a rigged race because all odds begin against us.

We can't do a thing, can't say a thing, and everything we need is controlled by someone else.

We begin hobbled, shackled, tethered and bound.

Not to mention the continual shattering of self-worth and sadistic cruelty that so many childhoods endure.

Not all lessons will be taught, but life won't miss a beat as to lessons we must learn.

Spiritual self-reliance, determined resilience and survival's desire, step in to provide us, if we allow, an inner compass.

I don't know that life is fair, for I cannot see how it possibly is, but I do know it is real, and we all run:

The Human Race.

Placing a bet on a life of worth after most childhoods,

are worse odds then taking a long shot on a Shetland Pony in the Kentucky Derby.

Did you ever consider, our little family, Humanity, an experiment to see if we ultimately survive?

A Cosmic wager on our Spiritual Evolution?

A long shot with staggering odds to see if we go from: Institutions of Religion -to- Spirituality of Individual. Politics of Power -to- People of Promise.

Aggression of War -to- Give Peace a Chance.

Division, Separation, Isolation -to- Unity, Togetherness, Embrace.

I, Me, Mine, -to- You, We, Ours. Catch this if you can.

Run little long shot.

Run!

True happiness is independent of temporary elation. True happiness is a lifestyle.

A choice.

A decision made, inside, regardless of circumstance outside.

A state of being.

True happiness is feeling blessed.

Temporary happiness is shallow, fleeting and conditioned. Like an addiction dependent upon outside conditions, it needs a fix to keep going.

True happiness encompasses strength of spine and tenderness of heart. It is unconditionally within one and unconditionally shared around one.

It cannot be bought, it cannot, be sold.

True happiness can only be gifted from inside.

∂∂∂∂

Risks in life are so adapted naturally, that every child on its own accord will willingly fall in its gleeful ability to walk. Every child will shake the constraints of its playpen. Every child will initiate sounds mimicking a spoken word. Every schoolgirl and every schoolboy will pursue unrestrained the innocence of puppy love.

Within a child, the innate ability to walk, easily overpowers the fear of falling down. Not a single child crawling upon its knees will ultimately shudder:

'Nope, not for me, might fall on my butt!'

The unknown, is not only natural, but life itself, continuously offers no other alternative.

How many Mothers have given birth before their first child?

What preparation is there for the actual enactment of the human species?

When death embraces, how is there to know the place of its arrival?

If the two absolute realities, that of being born and that of passing away come from a place of unknown, how can we be not suited as the ultimate takers of risk?

We are thrust into life arriving from who knows where and departing, to whither, we know not.

What is there regarding the in between that encompasses, the fear, the dread, the trepidation?

If we are blind upon arrival and blind into departure, can we not open our eyes throughout the in between?

If the unknown is much of what we are to experience, can't we know, within the known, that which is the knowing of itself?

Truly, we live our lives individually, standing on the edge of a precipice.

What danger is there in individually accessing life as our own?

How can we take life for granted and be terrified at the same time of being a risk participant?

Who are we truly that do not know right from wrong?

Who are we born without an inner ear?

Who are we that have not heard the whisperings of the guidance of ourselves?

Who can not sit and reckon within themselves the truth of a matter?

Those only, who do not risk. Those only, who must be told what to do.

The telling by one, taking advise from another, neither, having known the how of arrival, the where to departure.

Themselves, following the ruts on the road, left by someone else.

ᴊᴊᴊ

We have our thoughts, we have our opinions, we have our truths.

Yet there exists Natural Law.

It being unconcerned by our pondering perceptions and our arguments.

One profound awareness emerging as Natural Law, the world around us is reflected by the world within us.

We certainly are not in control of all circumstances, yet we have within us multiple options of how to react.

Have you ever considered life itself cannot be seen? Wind itself is not seen, but the blowing is obvious. You and I are a reflection of life.

All that we see, feel, and touch is a reflection of life. A manifestation of life. An effect of the cause.

We, in fact, do just that.

Affect the Cause. In return Cause the Effect. Let's begin by identifying who we are.

First we must challenge the myth that 'all men are created equal.'

We simply are not.

Humans are only equal in regard to what we need to physically survive.

We all need oxygen, water, food and protection from the elements.

Live or die.

This is all we need.

This is where our equality stops. Like snowflakes, no two human beings are alike.

Now us?

Who are we and what is there to encompass, if we

must intermingle, for we do, and purposely co-create, as we can, to become us?

Fully conscious, fully capable, fully present: You and I.

Let's begin by unraveling our layers of realities; physical, evolutionary and otherwise, that we were birthed in, birthed from, and are now surrounded by.

Spiritual, emotional, mental, physical, personal development.

Incarnate consciousness instated our embodiment of individual human life.

We were born in a time of history where all combined human consciousness and evolution had arrived at a certain state of being.

Our nationality and mixed nationalities carry, also, group consciousness. Our pieces of heritage are intermingled into our individuality.

Each nation carries risk, reward, opportunity, and constraint. We were birthed in a nation.

We were bred by our parents and we simply have to accept this.

Cursed it be or blessings to we.

We have become who we are by every single action whether voluntary or forced.

We have become who we are by every single thought, regardless of action, that we have accepted or rejected.

All our aspirations, imaginations, choice of activities, associations, prayer, swear and dare, have brought us to this present moment.

So here we are.

Seems hardly likely there has been another human created equal to you or I does it?

So be it.

In early childhood, adolescence and adulthood, there are countless circumstances, good, bad, parental upbringing, educational, immediate environment, siblings, associations, belief systems, a myriad of circumstances that will mold an individual.

Yet not one or all combined will make an individual.

We all peer through our own lens of individual identity. Two may think alike. Yet no two can think the same.

For a moment, yes. Much longer?

No.

The Ancient Greek Philosopher was not referring to the apparition we see in our mirror when he stated:

"Know Thyself."

Nature abhors a vacuum.

A space empty of matter, a state of emptiness or void.

This profound realization, in simpler terms, just means that any space open will be immediately filled.

We all know the term 'If one door shuts another one opens.'

This is the first and easiest step to changing our life. As a rule, we all try to add things to our lives and bring about positive changes.

That is fine, but it is far more effective to let negative behavior go, with the desirous knowing, that something more beneficial will manifest in its place.

This is the simplest way to begin creating the life we are desiring to make a way to exhibit itself.

Our mental space, intellect and thinking, are exceedingly limited in comparison to universal intelligence and the way of our Spirit.

The old saying goes, 'a blown 50 cent fuse will ground even the Space Shuttle.'

In reality, our habitual thought patterns and emotional behavior is that '50 cent fuse.'

We are all indeed intricately wired.

We all have our Achilles Heel.

We all have dark places within us. We all have unfettered access to the light, individual truth.

Children afraid of the dark, we have sympathy for.

Adults afraid of the light are no reasons for us to choose darkness.

❧❧❧

Keeping up with life, ironically, is not a matter of moving faster.

We actually initiate more productive activity and engage in more of what needs to be done, by simply, slowing down.

All of us are aware that the more our mind races the less we get done. Furthermore, a mind racing involves the body in a lot of frivolous activity.

A mind racing is a perfect vehicle for wasting time.

Living life productively is remarkably similar to breathing correctly.

Every athlete, singer, and those who practice yoga know one breathes from their diaphragm.

Slow deep breathing. This optimizes the specific activity.

Rapid mental surface activity can be compared to shallow breathing. Huge reserves of life stamina and natural ability simply remain dormant.

We can also use the analogy of a car.

The motor in a car is more relaxed and running cooler at 60 mph in its top gear of Drive, than it is at 30 mph in its bottom gear, racing in First.

More distance is being covered, yet less effort is being exerted.

The mind has a purpose, although, it is vastly over rated.

Mentally we cannot fulfill the functions that are the duties of the soul.

Our mind is like a steering wheel, we simply turn right and left, to keep us going in a proposed direction.

Our minds can be particularly harmful, if our mental processes go unchecked, they will indeed, take on a 'mind of their own.'

We then become a passenger, in *our own vehicle, out of control.*

It is a runaway mind that sends emotions awry, and the result is destructive.

Our daily mental process must be looked at objectively and through the eyes of mature accountability.

Mental activity can also be addictive.

Observe momentarily how our own mind can stay on a set pattern of thought, literally, year after year.

This being done without any input or even awareness.

We can wake up in the morning and engage in the same mental process that we lay to sleep the night before.

This is how the mind becomes extremely dangerous

and literally destroys our lives. This is how our mind takes on a life of its own.

We think we have to think, what we are actually being thought about, by our own minds.

Nothing is further from the truth. There are many things we cannot control, we can control our thoughts.

A mind racing about at break neck speed, should be dealt with the same as a child about to hurt itself, and that is to:

Simply put it in time out.

Day to day activities are all very necessary in terms of mundane responsibility.

There are two ways to approach them.

One of course is drudgery and lack. The other is a place of awareness that can actually change our surroundings. Truly, something as ordinary as washing dishes or running an errand.

We of course are there, whatever we are doing, or are we?

First we must separate conscious thinking from daydreaming.

Day dreaming actually escapes present time, diminishing and frittering away the solidity of reality around us.

Ironically, drudgery and lack, further plunges us into its own reality, the aftermath multiplying the same.

When it is all said and done, as much as we may disagree, it will not be coming down to what we've had, or have not had.

It will be the quality of existence, that which we house within our own consciousness, regardless of our environment, chosen by us, or imposed upon us.

Look at it through the eyes of a child and answer this question.

Does a poor child, nourished by an environment of love, tenderness, integral discipline, support and communication, have a richer life than a child who is rich, whose environment and parental relationship is lacking in these qualities?

Pretty clear to answer isn't it?

Long after adulthood we are continually raising the child within ourselves. We can only depend on us, to grow up.

That which an integral parent has to offer, regardless of our past, at a certain point, we must for true quality of life, offer to ourselves.

The first thing we have to be aware of, fully aware of, is wherever we go, there we are.

By this awareness it is easy to discover, we are constantly experiencing a relationship within ourselves.

We continually permeate the air within us, around us, with our relationship.

The relationship from us, to us.

In simpler terms, are we having a good day or a bad day? Impart unto ourselves the example of the richness of life the poor child is receiving.

Love, tenderness, integral discipline, support and communication.

Regardless of our immediate surroundings we actually choose emotionally and intellectually how we react to them.

Or we don't.

We are then, simply happened unto, by circumstance.

Have you ever noticed how children engage in activities fully present?

They may momentarily sit on the sidelines, but once committed, it is all caution to the wind.

In many cases, an adult will remain on the sideline while vicariously participating in the same activity.

Life is an activity. Life is fully present.

The entirety of life exists in complete wholeness, one split second at a time.

Life exists fully present in the present.

The entirety of nature's breath is fully inhaled and fully exhaled.

Spring, Summer, Autumn and Winter. Nature goes all out.

There is no holding back.

There is not a single leaf left on a tree in the dead of winter. The new buds of spring are fully present after a chilly, irreversible, long night of desolation.

A child likewise, innately knows the thrusts of new life.

Its direction is one direction.

What has happened to those of us who have survived winters unforgettable ache?

The chill that leaves the dead of night to give way to the dread of day?

What has become of us emotionally, mentally and spiritually?

Life is a perpetual cycle of birth and rebirth.

Yet who are we that endlessly drag ourselves about, sleep walking, in yesterday's corpse?

Why is it that we close the curtains within our hearts?

Why do we wallow in the ache of yesterday's winter, when springtime beckons?

We hurt our bodies, and on their own miraculous accord, they will heal.

Yet within us our emotions our hearts our anticipation for new life, many times we sorrowfully abandon.

Why?

It is a conscious choice you know.

There is a resiliency to body, likewise, a resiliency to spirit.

It amazes me how we will wash our bodies, put on clean clothes, yet leave our spirit unkempt in yesterday's garb.

We leave our heart, our soul, emotionally hobbling, festering an ingrown toenail that should have been plucked years ago.

Why?

Why do we teach our children to forgive, not only others, but themselves, when our own behavior can be utterly, emotionally, dishonest?

What is it in life that prevents our own living? Nothing.

Except for the totality of ourselves, or maybe just the little pieces that we refuse to let go.

Burst a smile on your face and have a laugh at yourself. Join me, have a laugh at me.

Observe a child at play. Become one.

~~~

If ever there is a job of complexity, responsibility, and the main derivative of humanity, it is Motherhood.

There is no greater gift to humankind than that of a Mother of Consciousness.

She, who has the ability to hold firmly, yet gently enough, to allow a child its own intrinsic response toward individuality.

There are no rulebooks or guidelines. A Mother does not birth herself, a part of herself yes, but even so, a stranger unto herself.

A child knows it is not one and the same as the Mother. A Mother discovers this continuously.

What greater sacrifice is there than to derive of oneself the living individuality of another?

What greater wholeness can exist when the bond is seamless, when the breathing of one, constitutes a breath, created by two?

What a child knows about its Mother is more than a Mother knows about her child, for children haven't learned yet to doubt what they know.

Truth is the most mysterious of observations, one can know another and the one that knows, knows, the other knows not.

Children being allowed their own intelligence will always know the Mother in ways, the Mother, knows herself not.

A child carries within its life currents, that which the Mother held, but a child knows, that which the Mother held, has to be let go.

Inclusion and simultaneous release are a delicate, continuously, transformative, mental, emotional and spiritual magnetic current.

A Mother cannot lead, and neither can a child, for both must lead and both must follow.

Yet there is intelligence, the Creator of the species, would imbue unto its own making, the advancement and protection of that species, and cradle it, in the hands of that whom it does, The Mother.

Reality Remembers Its Riddles and Rhymes

Day to day reality can be a most unassuming, and many times, unperceived phenomena.

We are akin at times to bouts of high drama, simply not being able to absorb, and positively process the mere reality of:

That which exists simply exists.

This is immensely valuable to understand.

Do your best to follow me.

Take something tangible, simply food and water. Both being a requirement for a physical body existence.

There is an expectancy and survival necessity for both substances to be there.

Yet food and water itself are not conscious of this fact, for example, corn does not grow with the consciousness of being eaten upon someone's table.

When planted in a field, it begins to participate in that which is life and draws to itself, elements for its own survival.

Unaware of its destined outcome, corn participating in our life substance by our utilization.

It can be eaten raw in the field and/or utilized in many ways, tortillas, cornbread, cereals etc.

Yet it can also be transformed into the making of a fillet minion by simply adapting it to another life participant.

Corn is unpretentious and comprehensive subject matter. It can be interactive in multidimensional ways,

simply by its transmutation, transformation, and adaptation as a staple for other life sources.

Now hold these simultaneous thought patterns:

A and B will be symbolically related to C and D.

Corn/food substance/clean water = Gratefulness/life sustenance.

Corn/food substance/clean water = Ungratefulness/starvation/death.

Conscious positive expectancy/undesirable outcome =

Anxiety/disappointment/victimized emotional behavior =

Field of all negative possibilities.

Conscious positive expectancy/undesirable outcome =

Acceptance/calm emotions/recognizing, That which exists, merely exists =

Field of all positive possibilities.

C and D are premised upon the fundamental truth: That Which Life is Merely Exists.

At any moment in past, present and future time, what here is, here/there/everywhere. Regardless what one may think, here is here/there/everywhere.

We may disagree on what that is, but still it is what it is, here/there/everywhere.

In other words:

That which exists, merely exists. OK.

In all circumstances, (C and D) there is a gap of time suspension, following the inhalation of life units, in regard to, conscious positive expectancy. Let's simply refer to this gap of time suspension as invisible uncertainty.

Invisible uncertainty:

Although we may be positively expectant, the outcome is not visible, until expectancy is manifested, physically or emotionally, desirably or undesirably.

Conscious positive expectancy, by its sheer nature, creates an elongation of concentrated emotionally stored, positive correlated life units.

Positive expectancy, by its very nature, creates a living emotional dam that is released, at the crossroad, where invisibility and reality meet.

Any parent with a 5-year-old child, promised an ice cream, and then refused, can relate, exactly.

The child is promised ice-cream; the child is in

positive expectancy. The child receives no ice-cream, and the emotional dam is released.

In essence, it is this emotional dam and currents of release that are being addressed here specifically.

For this subject, the circumstance of reality must be undesirable outcome.

Another example, a flat tire on a rainy night, no spare, no phone, on the way to an important occasion.

In other words, undesirable circumstances, where we are expecting a positive outcome and that does not transpire as anticipated.

These are gaps and voids in our lives, where what we have chosen as the outcome, is certainly not on our predetermined menu.

Another important point of consideration:

When the circumstance is desirable outcome, is gratitude equal to the positive expectancy, emotionally stored by the recipient?

A and B are exampled for purposes related to gratitude/ ungratefulness.

It is astonishing, how little materially we can have in life and yet remain eternally grateful.

Both are fascinating phenomena. These phenomenon being an engagement of living emotional units. Stored, electromagnetic, life substance.

C and D begin with the words, conscious expectancy and then follow equally and opposite.

These thought patterns must be taken in unison, although they are divided into parts of experiences, in emotional time (past, present, future.)

Pursue each thought pattern interactive in multidimensional awareness.

Begin with A and B, corn (food substance/clean water) Corn being utilized specifically as an example because of its wide ranges of uses in regards to transmutation/transformation and adaptation.

The field of all positive possibilities.

The point here is, emotionally, B, overwhelms, A, at large, where food and clean water are plentiful.

Human participate in the ungratefulness of that which is taken for granted. Yet there is an acknowledgment (life sustenance) in the body.

Although this acknowledgment (at its survival level) is non-dependent upon any range of emotional reaction.

The whole subject matter is rather consciously startling, for human survival is both dependent on food and clean water.

A, invites a far superior emotional/physical reaction, (where) food/clean water is scarce.

Life's emotional/spiritual day-to-day circumstances,

incidentally, share this same coincidence on more subtle levels.

Equally as noteworthy.

Life sustenance and/or emotional/spiritual/starvation/death.

This being the immense difference in the outcome in regards to the equal and opposite C and D.

Conscious positive expectancy / undesirable outcome =

Disappointment/anxious emotions /victimized emotional behavior =

Field of all negative possibilities.

Conscious positive expectancy/ undesirable outcome =

Acceptance/calm emotions /recognizing, That which exists merely exists =

Field of all positive possibilities.

There are many day-to-day activities, where conscious positive expectancy and desirous outcome must work in unison for one's survival, as in applying the brakes to our vehicles to avoid catastrophic outcome.

This example is self-evident, and we, in sudden emergency situations, are generally extremely grateful if our vehicle brakes are responsible for avoiding a collision.

Yet at large we are not conscious of our vehicles brakes, until negatively, when they must be replaced.

Let's move away from obvious eminent physical survival, into a more subtle multidimensional emotional/spiritual survival.

We have exampled the subject matter of A and B symbolically and can now begin to multidimensionally correlate, the other two, simultaneous thoughts.

In day to day life interaction there are many examples, where, if one of these interactions were to be removed, emotional outcome would be shockingly/disastrous, as for an example, the sudden death of a loved one.

Although, far to the extreme, this subject is more appropriately labeled grief. Yet can still be exampled. We can engage this subject more consciously by simply recognizing its severity of extreme.

Emotional/spiritual suicide is slowly committed, on a day to basis, by the inequality of relationship to C and D.

Thomas Edison attempted innumerable times to invent the light bulb.

At the end of each day's work of 'failure' he would remark, to those working with him, "We have discovered something very important today. We have discovered something that simply does not work."

In all reality the light had always been on for Tom, the bulb just hadn't lit.

This simple:

Acceptance/calm emotions/recognizing, That which exists merely exists, enabled Thomas Edison to continue pursuing the positive field of all possibilities.

Conscious positive expectancy is an individualized opportunity in which all are personally accessed to universal emotional life units. We actually 'inhale' and store these units within positive expectancy.

It is the aftermath, at the crossroad, where life's happiness and ultimate ability are determined.

It is this choice consciously, or unconsciously, that we choose in regards to an undesirable outcome.

This constant polarized positive/negative emotional/spiritual engagement is involved in all humans.

Individualized self-worth is determined by the choice at the crossroad (uncertain invisibility, meets certain reality) where the emotional currents are released.

Most importantly, we must experience gratitude regarding a desirable outcome of conscious positive expectancy. It reinstates the living emotional units (actual electromagnetic life substance) to be accessed later in day-to-day challenges.

This is especially in regard to unforeseen occurrences, and occurrences out of our emotional and physical control.

In reverse:

Anxiety/disappointment/victimized emotional behavior = Field of all negative possibilities.

These dissipate stored, positive conscious expectancy, life units. If this emotional release/behavior becomes habitual patterning at the cross road, where invisibility meets reality, life currents are short circuited in future, seen and unforeseen, challenging life circumstances.

If the choice at the crossroad becomes:

Acceptance/calm emotions/recognizing, That which exists merely exists.

The field of all positive possibilities becomes the integral life patterning of our emotional/spiritual behavioral countenance.

Whether it be consciously or subconsciously, we begin to access the greater part of our unknown intelligence. We begin to act instinctively on behalf of our best interest.

Furthermore, subconscious positive desires begin to

surface. A greater actuality of positive, emotional/spiritual and physical achievement becomes far more accessible than we had envisioned.

The field of all positive possibilities magnetically manifests on behalf of our best interests, bringing us full circle into Serendipity.

This manifestation takes place at a deeper level of soul initiation, accessing us, outside of ourselves, with inside of ourselves, simply being our Greater Good.

Adversarial circumstance does carry with it, the seed of equal and greater circumstance.

This is the balance in natural law.

This seed is planted at the crossroad of undesirable outcome, by initiating the thought form pattern of D:

Conscious positive expectancy/undesirable outcome=

Acceptance/calm emotions/recognizing, That which exists merely exists =

Field of all positive possibilities.

What is not automatically given by nature, is the interdimensionality to recognize, the equal and opposite beneficial circumstance. This is not a concern of nature; instead, nature's concern is merely existence.

What we must become aware of, embracing, is the transformation of any and all circumstances.

The rhythmic patterns of actual existence, knowing life exists, inter-dimensionally, regardless of perception. The mandates of our own consciousness.

Working the Streets of Soul Smarts

Be certain to love it when life is on a roll, be wise enough to know, it will always hit a rock.

Whatever we are doing or whatever we are pursuing, there are simply days, where all will go blank.

Motion stops and self-doubt awaits at the door.

In all actuality, these gaps must be recognized for what they are. They will always come along and are extremely valuable to a spirit aligned, goal fulfillment process.

These gaps are not here to be filled with self-doubt or an undoing of sorts.

For example:

When we travel across the country, clearly knowing and desiring the destination. Along the way, we may of course, become tired, anxious and impatient. We do not turn around in self-doubt, and fear, to go back for miles in the direction from where we have come.

We stop to rest.

This we know because it is a physical world we are traveling in.

A real car on a real road.

A real desire to go, the wherewithal to get there, and a real place to rest.

We are addressing days when we cannot emotionally and mentally put another foot forward.

Or if we become acutely sick.

These are days, or times within the day, when self-doubt, anxiousness or depression seem inevitable.

Let's first address mental processing for a moment.

Here is a simple analogy that I can count on happens to you:

When you hear a song on the radio, you know the name of the song, but for the life of you, cannot remember, it starts to drive you crazy, right?

This can be anything you can't remember, although, you positively know it. It also for some reason must drive you crazy.

When does the answer pop into your mind?

After letting the frustration go or momentarily having your anxiousness diverted.

Or even the next day.

But if you know it, you will always remember. Am I right? Yes.

This happens to all of us.

The mind directed with emotional intensity retrieves stored information for us all.

But also, like in this example, demands a gap or a void.

The answer bypasses our thinking and simply pops into our head.

So now we are exhibiting common sense in the real world, by taking a break along the way to a desired destination, and have an example, how mentally to get answers from our mind.

Physical reality and mental reality are quite frankly, very important, both to our sanity and to our emotional serenity.

We must realize, they are immensely limited in regards to our potential ability.

A highly stressed situation is far more intense, than not remembering a song on the radio, but still we have to 'let go to know.'

Circumstances we are terribly stressed about and in all actuality, don't truly know at that particular time.

Remember that the answer does not exist within ones mental framework because situations occur that we have never before confronted.

So in all reality, we do not have an immediate answer when it is uncertainty and fear of the unknown we are facing.

So where is and how do we get the answer? The right answer.

Our Spirit exists outside of our mental/emotional processes, yet, it still must coordinate with both to be utilized.

Our Spirit, or if you prefer the term Soul, is a part of ourselves, you want to be familiar with because if ever there ever was our better half, this is it.

The spirit must be invited to creatively co-create.

Financially it can be likened to an uncommonly large trust fund.

Mentally it can access the personal knowledge we need. Emotionally it brings serenity.

Yet It can only work with what it has available from the recipient:

That being you. This being me.

Our Spirit can also be extremely temperamental. This is from neglect and simply lack of trust.

It must operate personally through and within our own mental framework and emotional nature. Yet it can be enhanced, where it by passes both constraints, and simply manifests.

Early on in life, when we don't do what we know to be right, within ourselves, we begin neglecting our Spirit and pushing it aside and diminishing its potentiality.

When we are always questioning the answers we already know.

When we are continuously looking outside of ourselves for answers.

When we are taking adverse advice from others, against our own moral consciousness, Spirit is key.

If we continuously ignore it, it will crush us and bring us to our knees.

This will be our fate.

There are certain things in life we must count on. What I have just said is one of them.

Where is our Spirit?

What is it and what exactly is its function?

Let's begin with what we already know. What we have already heard.

Our still small voice.

Interestingly, it does not give an answer before we need one.

It operates with complete precision in ever-present time.

Spirit exists always and only Now, yet it has been around 'forever' and will go on without us.

My opinion of Spirit can be likened unto an ocean. It is accessible to vast reserves but initiates and coordinates within the small drop of water that we are. The small drop of water, microscopically, the entirety of the ocean itself is comprised of.

Spirit is also now and always now.

It cannot be stored. It cannot be preplanned. It always and only exists fully present.

Like oxygen, we simply cannot live without.

Like the oxygen we breathe, our Spirit is connected to a greater whole.

Each breath we breathe is one single complete breath at a time.

Think about it. Inhale/exhale. That is it.

We can't take it to the bank. We can't have it from yesterday; we can't save it until tomorrow.

We can't even hold it for a New York Minute. Try it, you know I'm right.

Even with an oxygen tank.

All we can do is utilize it, when we need it, and all we will ever need, is that one single breath, again and again and again.

Kind of scary if you think about it, right?

Yet we trust it always to be there and generally, it is, that is, until we get our heads stuck underwater!

Our Spirit, like oxygen, exists outside of us. Yet like breathing we make it intensely personal.

What is more, impersonal, yet more personal, than the air that we breathe?

Our Spirit permeates our mental body, our emotional body, and our physical body.

Very similar to oxygen.

We need oxygen to think, we need oxygen to feel and quite frankly we need oxygen to live.

Upon 'death' our Spirit leaves the body.

This is a fact, for the Spirit is fully detectable. It can be seen.

It is real. It exists.

It is the greater part of us because it is connected to the greater whole comprising of, as is the drop of water, in the ocean.

It is the only part of us that stays alive after we have gone.

It is the only part of us that was existing before we got here.

Amazing, because it exists and does for many, outside, within one, completely unknown to one's own consciousness.

How is this possible?

Before I answer that question consider this fact:

We can easily live a lifetime and never know our Spirit.

Yet our Spirit will thoroughly know the one, who has lived the lifetime, of unknowing.

This is where our minds, become belligerently overrated, as our soul source of intelligence.

This is where a human mind can be utterly destructive.

This is where a mind can and in fact does, leave us, singularly acting in its will, terribly far behind.

The greater part of us. The whole of us interconnected to the whole of all.

Nothing is more lethal than a mind that thinks it knows everything. The spirituality, the emotions, the flesh and blood attached to its needs.

The mind must know:

Spirit Knows.

If we rely on what we tell ourselves, well, let me ask you;

How often are you wrong and how often do you simply not know?

When one needs to know, when one truly needs to know, we must listen for our Spirit.

We must listen for our own still small voice.

If you and I were caught unaware in a critical challenge, with no clue where to begin, no memory to draw from being helpful, no understanding of what we are up against, Dumbfounded.

Literally blank and I suggest we 'think about it!' My friend, I have just suggested we pick up pennies outside the parking lot of our own Rolls Royce showroom, stack them together and begin counting bus fare.

※ ※ ※

Living an abundant, cherished life, is far simpler than most would know. In all reality, it is a simple act of perception.

The mere fact that we have conscious choice as to how we react to situations, outside of our control, is amazing all by itself.

A circumstance is simply, what it is, yet we have complete conscious choice as to how we react and perceive what is transpiring.

Life actually exists from the inside, that being, how we are perceiving, what is transpiring on the outside.

One man's ceiling is another man's floor, certainly, this is individualized perception.

Both existing in a perceived reality, yet, the circumstances can be identical.

One of the purest keys to all forms of treasured wealth is gratitude. Gratitude is an amazing, emotional stabilizer.

Gratitude cost nothing yet the investment in consciousness is priceless.

A life without gratitude would certainly result in a life of continual need.

Exhibit within ourselves a balancing act of consciousness where that which we desire, is balanced by the gratefulness of that which we already have.

Attracting natural abundance in all of its various forms is very simple. Be grateful to the natural abundance that exists within and currently around us.

Beneficial circumstances are attracted by engaging in this consciousness.

The simple act of breathing oxygen is natural abundance. All conscious breath can be transmuted circumstantially, into physical, emotional and spiritual manifestation.

Simply breathe in abundance and exhale gratitude. Nobody can prevent us from doing that.

All manifestation exists prior, either personally, or collectively, within Spirit before inhabiting reality.

How many of us face a circumstance of complete uncertainty, when doing something, the wrong thing is disastrous, only equal to doing nothing, which in turn is disastrous, and panic with our familiar inner voice screaming:

'I don't know what to do?'

Sliding deeper and deeper into one place of knowing and that place is, 'I don't know what to do!'

A relationship gone awry, divorce, deadlines out of control, fired, foreclosure, children choosing the wrong path, parents aging, or one left alone, natural catastrophe.

There are a million places where we simply go into uncertainty.

Let's be clear about this. This global mind consciousness is big business. The fear of the unknown, handsomely rewards the medical industry, insurance conglomerates, political landscape, security business, the war machine, religion at large, and that just mentions a few.

Life levels everyone's playing field with this reality. Money cannot buy ones way out of it. Neither can intelligence. Neither can belief, in whatever belief, you may believe in.

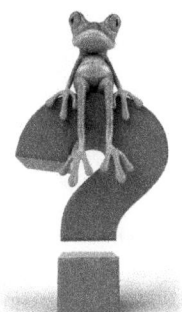

So often times, this is where Serendipity waits at the door.

In regards to complete uncertainty, how wrong is it, when all we know is, 'I don't know what to do?' Utterly wrong.

Nothing can be so horrifically wrong.

Nothing can be more dangerous. Nothing can injure one more. Nothing can harm the situation more.

Nothing creates more catastrophe and disastrous outcome.

How can we possibly know what to do about anything, when we only know, we do not know what to do?

Many wrong things will be done when coming to an agreement within oneself, 'I don't know what to do.'

Misery will always be prolonged. Many times we will hurt ourselves.

It's only natural to make the wrong design.

When faced with circumstances of uncertainty, only two things can happen:

We will become one with the circumstance, or, we will become one with the solution.

Knowing with complete certainty, we do not know, there is high probability we will become one with the circumstance.

On the other hand, knowing with complete certainty, 'All I know is I know,' there is high probability, we become, one with the solution.

We are either created by circumstance, or, we create circumstance.

Nothing else transpires.

Upon knowing nothing at all, the first thing we must know is:

'All I know is I know.

I may not know now what to do. I shall know what to do.

All I know is I know.'

Stand in utter fierceness in this truth. Do not waver.

No doubt. No shadows.

Once we have learned to access the truth within us, 100% of the time we will be right, there will never be an exception.

Before every break through is a breakdown. There is a gap, a void, a clear space for change to occur.

We do not know the right thing, when it comes along, when we have firmly established that we do not know what to do.

How many times have we done something only to say, 'I knew I shouldn't have done that?'

It is because we knew from the beginning, all along, that we didn't know what to do.

How will we know the right thing when it comes along, when we have firmly established, we don't know?

Every challenge carries within that challenge its very solution.

The solution may come from another.

The solution may come clearly out of the blue.

The solution may be totally unexpected, and nothing we had thought prior.

When one knows that one knows?

The knowing will surface in complete clarity. There is no emotion.

No thinking.

No spinning of the mind.

The solution appears as does a piece in a puzzle. It will not be forced.

It will fit perfectly.

༄༄༄

Life will never be fully productive and happy, until we learn to trust ourselves, and act upon that trust.

Life is a continual process of initiating and reacting to individual circumstances.

We must do both.

Life is continual processing, of decision-making, and either following through or not.

Trusting ourselves, is the inner knowing, that we will do right under any given circumstance and then doing it.

Nobody can, or will, always do right, but ignoring ourselves, not following our own intuition, ultimately leaves us victimized by the circumstance.

These circumstances occur in everyday affairs within our personal relationships, within our professional life.

Go back and remember situations gone wrong when they were either initiated, or reacted to under any of these premises:

'I knew I should not have done that.' 'I had a bad feeling.'

'All the signs were there, I kept ignoring them'.

'I was told by others, to make another choice, but I knew better.'

'I was told by others, to do right, but I didn't.'

'Why did I do the wrong thing, when I knew better?' If we cannot start here.

We can never start.

We can be certainly wronged by others, but we must accept responsibility for not following our own truth.

There is no one to blame but ourselves.

How can we not expect to be mistreated, stepping into a circumstance, we should not be in and further more explicitly being warned?

By who? Ourselves.

How can we expect a circumstance to go right when we do not listen to our own inner advice?

We must clearly accept responsibility for being wrong, when we know; we are either ignoring a circumstance or simply making a wrong decision.

Although once committed, there we are, hoping it will all be OK.

It is never OK. It is always wrong.

The price paid for little white lies to ourselves is crushing. Our Spirit, betrayed by our own behavior of ignoring what is right and what is wrong.

Justifying, being wrong in the face of inner truth, when we know quietly what is right, is no excuse to blame another.

This pure and simple is: Self Betrayal.

We have lied to ourselves, and we must realize if this continues, our Spirit has every reason to mistrust us.

We have trampled on our Spirit, and cannot expect our Spirit to be kind.

We would not think kindly on behalf of another exampling our actions.

How can we expect our greater selves to think kindly upon us.

Our still small voice becomes stiller, even more small. Be alert.

Be conscious. Be accountable.

When wrong and having not followed the above: Forgive yourself.

Start again.

We may be ourselves, but our Spirit, is in relationship with us.

Our Spirit holds us accountable whether we do or not. Spirit is all we have representing us.

Spirit also is Plaintiff. Lying to Spirit is perjury.

There is only one Defendant:

Guess who?

Be careful of getting trapped in the desperate valley of wanting. That awful place where 'everything out there' never seems to make it home.

Always know this truth:

That, which we are inside, magnetically draws what is 'out there,' to us.

In many ways life is a TV screen.

If we don't like the channel, simply change it.

Change it from inside.

Seriously, who can stop us? Who can think for us?

Who knows us?

Who creates our desires, who decides and discerns for us?

We all have responsibility to face, it's still best to be happy.

Happiness doesn't fall out of the sky. We pick it up off the ground. Abraham Lincoln said:

"We are about as happy as we make up our minds to be."

Pretty much says it, and you know of course you may offend somebody!

By being what? Happy?

Yep.

Life is a bit coy if we don't embrace it; it doesn't hunt us down to make our lives a perfect fairy tale.

Death is rather blunt and unconcerned with big hugs.

Life is a lot more friendly when we step back and acknowledge it.

It's like everything else.

It loves to have attention. It loves to be appreciated. It loves gratitude.

It loves friends.

In all reality life is competing against death, lack, need, and want.

It is competing against hopelessness and helplessness. Deprivation.

This is not life.

Death did not give birth to us. Life gets a bit lonely.

Do you know that hopelessly and helplessly wanting are two of deaths best friends?

It is doubting life, and honestly agreeing, that your want goes unfilled.

Which it does.

Because even if we get it, many times, it's not what we wanted.

Am I right?

Helpless and hopeless are terrific ways for a need to go unrecognized, because they are shunning the very substance that is used to fill that lack:

Life.

Everywhere is agreement.

If you agree to want, then want agrees with you. You team up as partners.

It's easier to have life, than want life, because life is already here.

Life is not something we have to dream up.

Helplessly, fearfully, wanting, pushes the very desire we are pursuing.

No matter what it is.

Hopelessly wanting is real popular these days and doesn't need any more attention.

Besides it doesn't have a single thing you want or need anyway.

Its job is straightforward.

It delivers hopelessly wanting, which in turn passes to fear, which is exceedingly busy if we don't get the things we must Have!

When we desire to have something, let's not sign our name on these black boards.

It's far better keeping our mental/emotional/spiritual balance.

Not yesterday, not tomorrow. Today.

This moment.

This will begin to multiply, even if it is remarkably small, what we do have.

Align yourself with this reality of thought substance.

Thoughts blended with emotion continually create our own reality.

Take stock in yourself.

We are far more capable than we realize.

It is rather futile continually putting our thoughts in the spin cycle of life's washing machine.

What then are we anxious for?

Circumstances to come out, clean, dry, and neatly pressed?

⁂

Why do we worry instead of simply trusting?

Why do we think we have to, as if it is our duty or a noble cause?

Would the airplane actually crash if we didn't constantly hold it up in the sky?

Or does the airplane, which is our life, have wings of its own on a predestined flight?

Are we secure enough to let go, to become?

Would it matter, if we knew that which we worry about, we ultimately attract?

That is if we are unlucky, because a great percentage of the things we worry about, never materialize.

Thank goodness, think of how many times we have been stressed over nothing.

Life instead pushes past our personalities, and

gives neither a tip of a hat, or polite curtsy to our concerns.

Do we recognize in this small moment of breathing, this microscopic incarnation that we have been borne within ourselves with infinite life experience, infinite memory, and infinite ability?

Look for example, how we react instinctively in emergency situations.

Yet we worry, and worry does carry a duty to manifest, an order from on high.

If we were to trust, would the outcome be worse than worry?

If we were to let go and become, would we fall recklessly within ourselves?

Worry circumvents the actualities, and potentialities that are longing to manifest in the now.

Worry agonizes us in the illusion: Tomorrow is more urgent than today.

Yet we can never actualize a time period outside of this immediate moment.

The entirety of a life can pass, blaming yesterday for a tomorrow that never transpires.

An entire life lived not, in the existence of: Now.

In its own explicit way, inner fear is a rejection of ourselves.

An inner timidity of the natural forces of our nature.

Fear is cowardice, slinking around cloaked in the darkness.

Courage stands naked in broad daylight.

Fear must be made into kindling, burning the fire of desire, yearning within us.

Fear focuses on have not, and allows not, to become.

Fear is the lion, tormented, by a thorn stuck in its paw. Afraid our own creativity will be rejected by others.

Our own individuality, becoming the muttering and parroting of the murmurs, of another.

Fear making us, a bird in a flock of feathers headed south, when our own wings desire pursuing north.

Before life is over, each one of us will experience, and for many of us, more than once:

The Dark Night of The Soul.

A place of utter desolation and sorrow, where the ego, emotions, and will, have blocked the essence of our pure being.

Our fire being starved by the lack of our own inner oxygen.

Our light, refusing to shine, by the will of our own darkness.

Emotional death haunts, and the Spirit of us willingly embraces.

We cannot fully live in the light of our own being, until we have bravely walked through the shadows, of our own darkness.

True sorrow for life lost, will offer the seed of humility for life to be relived.

We have within us, become judge, jury, plaintiff, defendant and we have found each part of us: Guilty.

We must make no excuse.

In the gallows of our own making awaits the noose where we shall hang.

Truth has been lies, and the circumstances that once haunted us, are now the realities we have feared, plunging ourselves into:

The Dark Night of The Soul.

Yet this experience can be made manifest into:

Our Brightest Morning. Make it be that way.

It is then we are in: The Valley of Decision.

All that we are, becomes mirrored at the crossroad, of all that we can become.

On the other side of this valley will be a new mountain and there can be a new us, awaiting, to take that first step.

Move pride aside.

Shut down the trembling ego. Quiet the emotions.

Remain humble in the pureness of our own light. This light is our very own.

This light is that which Life is:

Our only lantern, leading us home.

There is a creative stillness existing, lying outside the sphere of individuality, but we must go deep inside of ourselves to arrive there.

It can be likened to being inside of a building and descending many flights of stairs and then opening the door on the 1st floor to go outside.

We generally exist in a multitude of superficial places within our minds, creating mixed realities of our reality.

Questioning ourselves, arriving at the answer. Going in a direction then changing our mind. Back tracking to the original place.

Sitting and wondering what to do. Smoke and mirrors if you may. There is a way out of this.

We all have a calm within us that can be reached to enact a life of knowing, a life fulfilling, productive, desirous and enabling.

We must participate in this calm on a regular basis.

Money cannot buy this calm and the rewards of this investment are priceless. The creative stillness that lies outside of ourselves is different from inside.

This stillness is the womb of universal creativity and our descending within, down the many flights of calm, to this door of entry, leads us outside of ourselves to where the field of all possibilities exists.

The true art of creation awaits here.

The true art of creation exists within the field of all possibilities.

We can go, here, without leaving any place at all. Imagination diminishes into the stillness of nothing.

The stillness of nothing, resurrects imagination, into the reality of its own desire.

We must proceed bravely unto the still waters of our own soul, drowning without remorse, the pride within us. The pride that prohibits the life we desire to manifest, unencumbered, by our own weakness.

We must face our mirror squarely with our own unflinching eyes.

Not only to watch our backs, but to guide us in flight upon our own wings.

We must tread boldly into the back alleys and darkened paths of our own unknowing.

We must allow others to be, as we strive to become.

We must transmute death, into the yearnings of new life.

We must leap confidently, for it is always necessary, for the first steps of flight.

We must take time unto ourselves, for it is then, we welcome to know, who we have most neglected.

We must always know, to give to others, we must also take care of one.

We are that one.

Awaken from the ashes and stand with arms outstretched.

Cross the chasm that separates the fulfillment of our own desire.

Know that fear pales in the face of courage.

Fear hides in the darkened alleys of our minds, ready to pounce upon the trembling heart that slinks in the agony of its own pain.

Desire is the seed in the womb of the unknown. The invisible.

The unimagined.

Courage is valiant, the whole of the Universe smiles upon one, who recognizes within one:

The mystery of reality enveloped by one. The Art of Creation.

Becoming What Is Because We Already Are

We cannot know life until we know death. We cannot know love, until love knows not. We cannot know one, until we know two.

One plus One.

꜄꜄꜄

Emotional longing is a phenomenon. I ask myself.

Is it me within me, I'm reaching for, in my outreach for another?

Is it me that I run from, when I push others away?

Do my enemies show me my own blindness, gaps within my own being, that long in the night and hide away from the approaching Sun?

I've always wondered about my friends and my enemies. Because rhythmically they are the same people.

Even if they take on different bodies, throughout life, they are the same people.

I wonder at times who I value most within the same person.

One, who is my friend, or the other, my enemy?

Many times, I've concluded it is the enemy, who my friend, has become.

It is because, at times like these, they show me a place inside of myself, where they are right and I am wrong.

As hard as it is sometimes, I love to be wrong. I love to see the world through others eyes.

Those times when it comes to me, when it is another vision, and not my own, that is clear.

These are times when I love my friends to be my enemies.

These are times where either I grow anew, or hold on to a blossom the bitter frost has bitten as it blows abandoned into the wind.

When your candle has flickered and its flame blown out by the winds of strife.

If perchance, one comes along and offers the flame of themselves to light your darkened path;

Tread boldly.

Those times, we cannot light the flame within.

This is why friends must be chosen wisely, for they inspire, or they make one less.

For we can give unto another, until, we have given ourselves away.

No wood to put upon our own fire, yet we have left another, burning bright.

This is why we are in a world, of many, as we select the few.

It is those few that we must ask ourselves, is our giving equal to our receiving?

Are we being taken, to give ourselves away?

It is always those few that revolve our own lives.

It is always those few that make us, available, to ourselves.

Those few that separate and discourage.

Those few who encourage and we become more able. Those few that we build our lives around, the life we build within ourselves.

True friends are building blocks within our own lives. We become building blocks in return.

Treating each other as ladders to climb, and paths to tread upon, we become rungs for another, and our countenance is soiled by the tracks, we have left for another, upon our own backs.

True friends are nuggets of gold, separated and cherished, from the sand of life.

Losing ourselves in another is a frightening occurrence.

This happens within a myriad of different emotional conditions.

It is always related to an inequality within a relationship.

We simply emotionally, or otherwise, are giving in a manner where there is no equal and opposite balance.

We give and give until that which has been given away, has taken away, the individuality of our emotional core.

This unselfish outpouring, with no reciprocation, leaves our heart starving, isolated, vulnerable, and ultimately shattered into many pieces.

When and how do we stop and recognize that this is transpiring?

We do not.

Not the first time.

We can only recognize after this has happened. This is a particularly delicate reality because inevitably, there is a hardening and a heart to be made wise.

In this case, what part of the heart hardens, and what part will become wise?

The part of the heart that has the ability to love unselfishly?

The part of the heart that objectively recognizes an inequality, when one loves unselfishly?

Let it be both.

Transmuting sorrow and emotional loss is loves greatest lesson.

Bitterness and scorn, are loves lessons, lost.

❧❧❧

Beware the sacrificial sentient of servitude, leading down the paved roads of submission, past road signs of sleeping senility.

Acting in subservience, causing our point of center to be off balance.

One end of life's teeter-totter, remains, firmly stuck upon the ground.

Circumstantial reality, placing one abruptly participating in a smorgasbord, where food for life is digested, yet it neither nourishes the body or the soul.

The clang of alarms jarring our senses, and overruns of time, that leave us panting merely for the recycled oxygen of another.

Negligent actions, on our plate of life, leave us bewildered, overloaded, and our soulful stomachs burning with fire.

Still the voice of the small whispers.

The call of the wild haunts footprints, faded on the road less taken.

Miracles in our pocket yearn for the sunlight of a breath from our own consciousness, to activate our reality, to mirror the landscape of our minds filled with mystery, magic and the imaginable.

Invoke the resilient nature of our spirit to emerge from a body, drowning, and helpless beneath life's swift and dangerous rapids.

A body buried beneath the crushing waters.

Refuse to muddle in distant sorrows, forgotten chances and breathe only the purity of a Sun, that, even in nights darkest moments, forgets not to rise fearlessly again in the morning.

We are the seeds of humanity, and we are many, who have been planted for this task by the great caretaker, of our human garden.

This is the core of our value.

This is that which is within us, that changes eternally, and ever remains the same.

This is our mark of mystery.

This defiance, never to leave ourselves defenseless, in the muddled madness of those marching mindlessly into their own mirrors, of vanity, mayhem and mundane.

Through it all, we must have agreement. We must elicit.

We must share the life of each other for our own to be sustained.

We must have each other, to echo the haunting of our silence, for even the whisper of desire, goes unheard without the consciousness of sound.

Let each moment rush in an octave of one's own originality.

The anxiousness of adrenaline awaiting only to press our lips upon a trumpet as our eyes stare unflinchingly at:

The Walls of Jericho.

Yet even perched precariously upon those menacing walls, resides the Humpty Dumpty, within us all.

The sound of our trumpets, will invoke the inevitable fall, and neither all the kings' horses, and all the kings men, will put us back together again.

Ourselves must put us back together:

Anew.

Loving another and not leaving ourselves behind, is a challenge we all face.

Wholeness of being, giving and receiving, is not

presupposed taking in consideration, infancy, when we only know to demand and take from another.

With all due respect, it is our survival at stake.

This may at first seem unjust, but does offer within one's own consciousness, an invitation of desire, for emotional and spiritual outreach to begin occurring.

Women by nature, are more equipped for selfless, physical and emotional giving, the continuation of the human species is dependent on this.

Apart from this immediate consideration, all relationships are a varied and fascinating phenomena, a maze of mirrors within ourselves.

Relationships enacted even upon early adolescence, begin to mirror ourselves, unto ourselves.

We begin finding wholeness within ourselves, as we mirror and intertwine with others.

These relationships are not subject to other human beings only, for they occur within our interaction, with animals and nature as well.

Consider this:

Within us are life units that can be likened to an ATM card that we simply draw upon daily.

Yet there are limits.

We then invest these living units within ourselves and each other, and the question of course, is how do we know if we are investing wisely?

How and why do happy marriages end up in, bitter, prolonged, divorce?

Is it just me or does it seem odd to you, that in many cases, the one, who one, would take to love the most, becomes the one, who one, most bitterly hates?

Interesting, because something must have gone dreadfully wrong!

Marriages are institutions of human.

No one can predetermine, and neither would God expect one to know how another will become or act, as life continues to transpire in day-to-day fashion.

If marriages were ordained by God, no man, would or could, tear asunder, what

'God has joined together.'

If one remains individualized, that is staying one within our self, yet coming together with another, a perfect marriage, if you will, occurs.

Many times when we are emotionally or spiritually stolen from, we have just sacrificially, or may I say recklessly, thrown these parts of ourselves away.

Another has not received them, for another was not looking to come into an agreement with them.

What is best for one, based on individualized wholeness, becomes the best for another because no usurpation transpires.

As with a preset daily cash advance limited ATM card, no indebtedness can occur.

Our relationship becomes honest and real, as likened to spending our own money in an integral ongoing fashion.

This money of course is not only money but emotional and spiritual life units as well.

These cannot be fleeting gratuities overcome by romantic and sexual euphoria.

Unfortunately, we cannot expect another, always to do the same.

Yet, it is our right.

It is our emotional, mental, physical and spiritual responsibility.

It is our right always to choose.

It is our right to act upon unforeseen change. It is our domain.

When emotional/spiritual indebtedness steeply occurs within ourselves, on behalf of the actions of another, it is wise not to sell the farm.

When the beckoning within us, begins the leaving of another:

It is one step forward, to the better one walking.

Miraculous, the yearnings of a heart unhealed, carrying itself, in a manner that pursues its own right to life.

Caring neither what the mind thinks or does. Listening to no other voice except its own. Without reason or indifference.

Pursuing and expecting no other way except the right of way.

No excuses.

Looming larger than life.

Retaining the only image in the mirror. Relinquishing no fight and accepting no reason.

Longing and assuring a path will prevail. The heart knows no fear.

Its sea, upon which its own sail is set, listens to no

other voice and the wind it makes for travel, is its own.

It becomes one with the sea and drowns the water it breathes.

One with the rocks it is crushed upon. Food for sharks that tear at its underbelly.

It transmutes itself and transforms along its way. It is one and then another.

Yet it remains whole unto itself.

The pureness of a heart can never vanish. It can blow away, but invisible, it is not.

It can be trampled upon, prey, for another.

Its strength lies in its own weakness, to never, let never, say never, again.

꜀꜀꜀

If you are observant, there are times and continuing of times, when all defenses within the ego and the scarred emotional bodies of pain are suddenly confronted by the light of our own spirit, and vanish instantly.

The ego is back of course, yet emotional pain can be transmuted.

In these moments, both can be less, and life within can be more.

There must be an openness to embrace the unknown.

Shattering illusions and the transparency of reality beckons our own essence of truth.

Ecstasy and sorrow intermingle, separately. Pulling in opposite directions.

Pulling apart ourselves, pouring into the wholeness of our self, yet awaiting, is a new self we perceive to be no one at all.

This is when not to hold on. This is when only to let go.

These moments offer ourselves to our greater self.

All that we think, all that has been known, suddenly is the utter knowing of not.

Stepping from our past shadows of delusion into ever-present reality, offering ourselves anew.

Shattering into pieces, the wholeness of ourselves, leaving the pieces to fall and burst forth as seedlings in spring.

᠉᠉᠉

Understanding and embracing life fully can never be obtained until one has been purged by sorrow.

Sorrow has been transmuted into joy.

Joy is unconditionally shared with others.

It is through sorrow that the ego is shattered and lays waste.

It is through sorrow that the selfish I within us becomes the unconditional we unto another.

Sorrow is the key to humility.

Humility is the key to a life unfettered by vanities and preconditions.

Sorrow is the field where all life players are leveled. Sorrow is death's shadow.

It must be embraced. It must be endured.

It must be transmuted.

Sorrow is the key to unconditional happiness. Sorrow is also where bitterness, and scorn ripen. Sorrow is the ultimate, 'No Pain No Gain.'

Once that marker has inevitably been laid down, that will be where all true emotions pivot.

Life itself is continuously fluid, ever changing and always remains in present time.

However, our emotional nature does not have to abide by these laws.

It is unfortunate to find ourselves in an emotional situation, selectively aligning truth, justifying holding firm our own cherished position.

Relationships will always hit a crossroad, where non-emotional objectivity should be considered.

Based on one's own cognizance, in what manner is the relationship, if at all, worth continuing?

To answer this question:

Let all the rubbish go within the relationship and take a look.

Let all the goodness go within the relationship and take a look.

Take a good look:

What remains clearly to be seen?

It will always have been our last little bit, our continued last effort, our eternal persevering.

The start of an extraordinary new morning.

The close of a full day honored. But isn't that what life is anyway?

The ultimate embrace for existing now?

The ultimate reality in moving forward?

When we hide away in fear of this, it is then we work to prevent the entire natural rhythm of the way things truly are.

The whole of the Universe is eternally growing, constantly changing, in continual motion.

Complaining about life is a sure fire way to make it more difficult.

But why do that?

Growth, perseverance and challenge, is our entire reason for living.

We won't be blowing our horn at death, so we might as well, give a hoot about life.

I mean it won't be the dying that is going to kill us. It will have been our lack of living.

Look within ourselves at all the joy lost through worry, anxiety and continued fretting.

When it is said and done, won't we question why we did all that?

Won't we ask ourselves why we made it all so difficult?

Why we worried, today, over endless things that never happened?

Why we worried about tomorrow and sure enough, it arrived to worry again, about a tomorrow that never came?

We were exhausted from what? Continually beating ourselves up!

We couldn't live productively and life continually eluded us?

Spending our days, too little too late, laying down,

letting go and running away to arrive where we didn't want to be?

Doing what?

Escaping within the shadows of an existence, fear based and fear bound?

Hiding away and holding our head in our hands, hoping and praying a miracle will fall from the sky?

We are that miracle.

We have fallen from the sky. Today.

A little piece of heaven on earth.

Accepting a difficult situation is the first key to changing it.

This may sound odd because why would we accept something, somebody, or a situation that we prefer removed or changed?

Acceptance takes resistance away.

If you have ever been swimming and are caught in a whirlpool, the first thing you do is relax and be pulled under, then swim out.

In other words, Don't fight the current.

The same when driving, our car goes into a slide, we let go of the wheel, actually turning into the slide.

Relaxing and allowing natural momentum. Don't resist, Let Go of the Wheel.

We gain control by letting go. Life is remarkably similar.

Consistent fighting creates continued resistance and the fights are never over.

If we are not able to dodge the bullets in life, which many times we can't, we must let the bullets pass through us and not get stuck within us.

Releasing aggressive restraint on situations and circumstances, simply accepting what, IS, puts into motion, passive withdrawal and the desired outcome of change.

Constant turmoil over a desired change will always push the outcome of desire away.

Embracing through acceptance that which we wish to let go is a simplistic way to create an extremely effective release.

Through this reversal of mental and emotional thinking, the turmoil within a circumstance will actually slip away and the solution will begin to surface in complete clarity within ones consciousness.

Very simply stated is this awareness: That which we resist, persists.

Truth is a compelling perception regarding traumatized emotional circumstances.

Facts of course remain unalterable, the actual logistics of a situation.

But are not somebody else's feelings fact?

There are times, within the intimacy of a relationship, episodes will occur where both parties remain in direct conflict.

Where in reality, the facts being asserted one to another, are actual truths based upon two opposed emotional responses to a circumstance.

More harm and misunderstanding is done, when people go round and round, over what a person has factually done, or not done.

Emotional traumas will always loom largely over any underlying, objective, cold, hard, facts.

What is true, regardless of fact, is how a person feels, about what, has transpired.

Traumatized feelings can often result in a decision held firm and many times irreversible.

Intimacy ultimately disintegrates by simply not being acutely aware, and compassionate, to this understanding.

In relationships worth preserving, it is immensely vital, to recognize the emotional truths of another.

War between roses, does not have to leave, either, or both, barefoot among the thorns.

After we have been 'hurt by love,' our hearts can never fully open anew without full emotional closure.

Emotional closure is when we begin reuniting within ourselves, compassionately and responsibly to regain our wholeness.

Full emotional closure will always encompass unconditional forgiveness.

Holding ourselves accountable, another accountable, and forgiving both.

In regard now to relationships encountered and endured by choice.

One cannot abuse one, if there is not another to be abused. One cannot neglect, abandon, betray or leave one in sorrow, if there is not a recipient for this to occur.

Our first love is always remembered, because our first love, begins, unencumbered.

Every love can be as our first love, if full closure, can be understood and achieved.

Life is a continual cycle of beginnings, fruition and finality.

Even within a permanent, loving, evolving, relationship, these cycles exist.

Closure within a loving relationship is a two-part consciousness:

Forgiveness and responsibility.

These two parts must be enacted unconditionally. One forgives another; the other is responsible not to repeat the action. This results in mutual agreement, love and respect for each other.

Two must understand, that one cannot be all to another, therefore, mistakes and shortcomings will intermingle with growth and positive attributes.

Relationships are a two-lane highway.

Loving relationships require equality of compassionate consciousness.

Loving relationships require continued equality of respect and agreement.

If not, relationships become a one-way street, inevitably, a dead end road.

Soulful, loving interaction lost, mutual respect gone, togetherness for one has become separation for both, and two people live lives of emotional estrangement.

Two people isolated in their protection of themselves.

Roles are generally assumed and structured. One being dominant the other submissive. Inevitably one breaks away. Wounded, bitter, broken, is one or both hearts.

It will be circumstance due to the last straw.

It will be tolerance shattered beyond our threshold. When this occurs, we have left the other, and now must seek emotional closure within ourselves. To live fully again.

To love fully again.

When hatred is held against another hatred is held within ourselves.

When bitterness, disappointment, rejection, abandonment, sorrow, and all emotional pain are held against another.

The same remains within ourselves.

These emotions, will continually bind to ourselves and invariably, recreate in an entirely, new relationship, the identical circumstance.

We must unconditionally forgive ourselves, and another, thus letting the past go.

Forgiving one of wrong doing and repeating the same mistakes, are entirely, two different subjects.

Justice and accountability must go hand in hand, with forgiveness, and emotionally letting go.

When unconditional closure is not attained, these broken parts of our heart will begin intermingling into a new relationship.

Rebound relationships are a perfect example of this.

They are doomed to failure because we are attempting to find closure in another who is not responsible. Or two are coming to together to fight a fight that is not finished.

Entering a new relationship without first closure on the old, many times we begin treating the other, how we were just mistreated. This can be wholly unconscious.

In other words, rebounds and unfinished closure result in role reversal.

A continuing from another, the abuse one has just, or so it seems, released oneself from.

Relationships, beginning again, without forgiveness of ourselves and emotional closure on another, become an endless spiral of either, chasing, or running away, from what we have just left behind.

Upon closure, maturity and responsible compassion develop within the heart of the recipient.

Two healed hearts come together, with an innate emotional, spiritual maturity, an unfulfilled longing:

The seed of desire for love to be nurtured.

This relationship unfolds the realization of love. Love is then not fallen into but risen unto.

Two hearts thus cleansed.

Love begins anew.

If we were aware the power of forgiveness, we would do whatever necessary to make it happen.

Forgiveness is a phenomenal key for inner growth and life will assure no shortage for inspiration.

Being stepped upon by another is far less tragic than being stepped upon by ourselves.

Forgiveness is neither frailty, feebleness, nor forgetfulness.

Forgiveness instead, is us rescuing ourselves, from emotional fatality, fierceness in the face of finality.

Why?

That which has happened wrongly by another cannot be undone. If it can be prevented from happening again, in all seriousness, it must. But it cannot be taken back.

Yet it can be transmuted, it can be transformed, it can be aligned for inner allowance.

It must be, or it will instead, block, negate and prevent our personal growth.

It will seed within its core a contempt within our own condition.

Forgiving another has nothing to do with the myriad

of options; another may or may not take in regards, to the one, who has forgiven.

Yet refusing to forgive another, sets up the re-occurrence, of the same.

Refusing to forgive, refusing to let go, emotionally imprisons within us the act of transgression.

So

Two wrongs will have been committed. One upon us by another. One within us by ourselves.

༄༄༄

Sometimes it is hard to recognize everything works together for our own good, yet it is never hard to realize, if this is what we know.

Life adhering within the framework of a static consciousness, will always leave behind, in its wake, the tatters of a frayed reality.

Absorbing and transmuting, not only the darkened places within us but also the light, will show us, even upon the steps of a misguided path, our natural way home.

It is not only ourselves, but it is the others within us, that we use as oil within our own lanterns.

We can only love another with the love we have for ourselves.

The reality of our lives, within our wholeness and our strength, is all that we can offer another.

We can only reach out for life, with hands that give back for our own embrace.

This, is becoming our own best friend.

Becoming the best friend, to another.

༄༄༄

Observant, skeptical reservation, is a prudently thin line to tread upon.

It is necessary among the waters of life because piranha feed upon the remains dropped from the mouths of sharks.

Life is strewn, with the innocent, the gullible, the Pollyanna.

Yet agreement, within its simplest terms, is the single prerequisite, the single source field, not only for the sublime in miracles but also in a day-to-day world of manifestation.

Yet actual agreement between two or more can be undeniably elusive and miraculous in its own making.

Agreement is where there is no doubt, no hope, there is no faith, there are no gaps in consciousness between those coming together.

This frequency or spiritual tone of duplicated resonance, facilitates on its own behalf:

The Actual Art of Creation.

Agreement cannot be taught. Agreement cannot be learned. Agreement is something that happens independent of thought.

Agreement is an evocation of the spirit. Agreement is achieved by the absolute knowing of one to another.

One may know first and another can discover afterward, but the knowing must be identical, and it must connect momentarily, simultaneously.

Identical in spirit.

Spirit that lay outside of perception and consciousness. A knowing that does not consist of desire.

A knowing that is immovable. A postulate of absolute.

In an instant, all work is done.

The rest is simply an out picture, a download, the unloading of a truck full of produce.

Participating afterward in the agreement becomes a choice because, in all reality, the work of spirit has been complete.

Agreement on its own accord is spontaneous combustion.

Agreement is why miraculous happenings happen instantly.

Agreement is how inventions are complete in the mind's eye of an inventor.

Agreement is how a novel exists before a single page has been written.

Agreement having been achieved, work if it can be called that, is an effortless integration within the fluid forces of life that collate around that agreement.

Agreement is communication unspoken. It is resonant of duplication.

Agreement truly is: "As above so below."

It is within one, and it becomes one, with another. All human emotions circumvent agreement.

For agreement is without emotion and happens within the still of the calm.

Agreement is to know without desire. Knowing without anxiousness. Knowing without faith.

Agreement is ultimately the God within us, exampled by the story of God's own act of creation:

"And God Said."

Agreement happens and continues to happen from multitudes of people who will never meet.

Agreement is duplicate spiritual alignment regardless of culture and language background.

Agreement can happen spiritually, one from another, through aeons of time.

Agreement, through spiritual and emotional resonance, connected at the absolute place of still, is the single most potent force field utilized within the supremacy of creation.

Agreement is not wanting something. Agreement is becoming something.

Wanting is a gap that must be null and void for actualization to appear.

Agreement is outside the human perception to think.

Agreement rests inside the will of Nature's Law to know.

)))(

Reality is an intriguing observation because the truth is, we do not see life as it is.

We see life as we are.

Proof of this exists in the fact that two people can see the same glass and one will see it half-full and another will see it half-empty.

Relationships with others, take on a whole new meaning, when you realize that everybody, in their own way, are fighting their own personal battles.

We must know this.

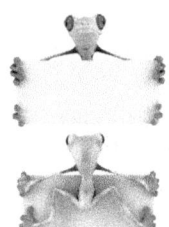

When we look at another regardless of what we see outside of themselves, there is the frailty of their own weakness, within themselves.

A mirror we all peer into, where our insecurities loom large, yet others recognize not.

One can only be humbled embarking into the mystery of personal love.

The mystery of universal love.

Love is actually an allowance for another to be who they are.

Yet, at the same time that allowance coincides, who we actually are, within ourselves.

This allowance intertwines to that which we aspire, within another, mirroring the highest ideal of ourselves.

Love is not a feeling.

Though many feelings are stimulated by love.

Love can never harm, because love itself cannot be harmed.

Love is not an action.

Although one will act existing in loves sphere.

Love can never be deprived of life, because love creates the living.

Love cannot be a sacrifice, because love cannot take away.

Love can intermingle with, that which love is not, yet love remains whole unto itself.

Love can never be taken from one, because love can only give.

Love can never want, because love is never in need.

Love cannot be lonely, because love itself is not alone.

Love cannot demand, because no demands exist within love.

Love exists outside of condition, stipulation, and requirement because love exists unconditionally, without harassment and free unto itself.

Love can be given, to one, be given to many, be given to all.

Yet love does not need, the one, the many, neither the all.

Embracing a relationship, as an exploration of our potentialities, is where love meets life walking hand in hand.

This relationship is not a tug of war where one is left the victim, but a tug of heart, where both become the victor.

Two mountains to climb are not one valley of despair.

Two bumpy roads do not become one broken pavement.

This relationship is not built upon the strength of one, but upon the unity, of two.

Pulling apart comes together, in sewn new fashion. Isolated paths merge upon love's road of togetherness.

Vulnerability of the heart does not weaken the strength of the soul.

Apart from each other, shares, to come together. Two mirror the best one can be.

Putting one first does not leave the other behind. Two become one and give to each other.

Life within love stirs potentiality alive. For one does not rule.

Two together reign.

᠈᠈᠈

Awaken to life, dizzy and alluring, this sensual sea of water that invites us home.

Awaken the intoxication of the rush of life from unexplored places.

Awaken a calm that soothes our heart like even a rock of warmth beneath the belly of a lazy lizard.

Life radiates our being and all that we muse. Make manifest for us, and offer, and offer only.

Courage never rests.

Malice be not and neither be envy.

Embrace life as we offer our heart, to a greater heart, and our soul, to a greater soul.

Give way our body to victory.

Relax our will as nature unfolds our precise plan and offers a garden that is full.

For we must decide and we must remove what is excess.

Come to life's fullness and lie upon the bed of invitation. Fill every untended and arid place in our soul.

Meld the splintered pieces of a heart abandoned and now fill our bodies with life's living ecstasy.

Know from afar life has come to us and know from within, life awakens, inside of us.

Know the firmness of a steady gaze. Know the right of will.

Nature has given us instruments of strength, and souls that guide unerringly.

Fear no fire and fear no fall. Abandon not our right to choose. Our will to decide.

Our decision for fight or flight. Our decision to love one another. Our decision to let one go.

Our decisions, soothing a heart, directed by the choice of our own soul.

Be more unto ourselves, and be unto life, flaming a fire where no coldness can enter.

Build within us a home where we reside in our own fullness.

Discover the magic of our soul, the readiness of our Spirit.

Be unto ourselves vulnerability protected, sensitivity nourished, tears of joy that wrap around a soul of strength.

Be ever held tightly in Love's womb and bring to ourselves fierce adventure.

Give to ourselves wings of flight, and tarry if we may, but never tarry, if we must.

ᴊᴊᴊ

Life is our main and always, renewable, recyclable experience.

Throughout life's entirety is continual change. Nothing stays the same and all life remains in constant flux.

Even those who attempt to hold things in their proper place, must realize, change will occur, either inwardly or outwardly.

Whatever you are cherishing, whatever you are holding onto tightly, it will change.

For better or for worse, either, or both.

We always find time to do and care about that which is most prominent.

We always feed the essence of ourselves into others and circumstances that fill us with the needs, or perceived needs, we value most.

Knowing this allows us to look about our life to see what and who we have drawn unto ourselves.

We must know, those who we love, that which we do, we must know, this will always:

Change.

Change can be subtle, imperceptible and go unnoticed. Change can be dramatic, immediate and explosive.

Life actualizes and formulates through awareness, pure intention and goal deliberate activity.

Life does the same through ignorance, neglect and unintentional activity.

These characteristics, equal and opposite, make for continual change.

All of nature, all relationships, all circumstances, situations, every facet of life, if ever you forget, change will remember, that you will not.

Embrace change. Honor change. Rust never sleeps. Sleep never sleeps.

Every rock in the field, though imperceptible, is in continual motion.

Everything that was, no longer is. Everything that is, will no longer be.

Only one thing remains the same and even it: Changes.

❧❧❧

Join life in a love that is inseparable and a friendship that is joyous. A brand new start and a release of yesterday's sorrow.

Join life in forgiveness for she recognizes that each one of us are human with frailties and weakness.

Join life in letting go and letting be.

Life of gentle strength and tender heart. Where dreams are realized and passions expressed.

Where goodness surrounds us and angels administer blessings of joy.

Where we mellow and find comfort in the realities of today.

A love to share entirely as life runs through us. Nurture

life to blossom in ways that are her very own. A life of honesty and continued sharing.

Remember always to love her gently.

Join life in change and growth, in laughter and embrace, in tears when they must fall.

Join life even now after all you have been through. You only have each other.

꩜

The wonderment of life is always here, regardless of disappointment, heartbreak, sorrow and loss.

Like our best friend, continually beckoning unconditionally, 'Awe don't worry about it; shrug it off, come play with me.'

Every day is an entire lifetime, a complete cycle of new birth.

Pure unadulterated invitation.

Everything that is, goes, comes, goes, comes again and goes away.

This is the beauty, so jump in, add, embrace, give to another, transmute and transform.

We all go through spells of transformation and metamorphosis.

We are part of nature. This is what nature does. Life, death, rebirth.

Again and again and again. All in one year.

All in one month. All in one day. Today.

This moment.

Objective consciousness is invaluable.

Recognize this natural cycle of actions in all facets of life because regardless of recognition, this is, what happens.

This is what reality is.

This magical mystery of continual change. Euphoric elation.

The melting of our emotions.

The panic and our heart in our throat.

The close calls and trapped on the tracks of an oncoming train.

Nobody can say it's not real visiting this little piece of Earth, Fire, Air and Water. This grain of sand in our vast universe.

Step aside momentarily and see for yourself, perhaps, in a way, we have all done everything we are doing now, before.

The physical circumstances are rearranged, but look at the emotional, mental and spiritual intonations.

We get through it all no matter what it is. Until we don't.

But even then we still do, we just may not know it yet.

)))⟩

All we can be is all there is left to be doing. Today dances that distance of illusion.

Tomorrow is remarkable because actually today participates in creating it.

Even less mysterious, today will make yesterday. Yesterday, today was tomorrow, see for yourself. One day at a time.

That pretty much sums it up. If there is another way

I am open to suggestions.

A Kiss or Frog Legs in the Soup?

Fortunately we are not living in the Dark Ages because I can assure you, my next observation would meet me face to face with, well, I'll let you read for yourself.

Secondly, I was probably on my way to a kiss, but my fate with many readers will now be the pot of boiling water!

You can see I am adequately handsomely prepared!

In all seriousness, nearly single handily, it has been Truth to Power that has brought us to a new age of enlightenment. The power has been in the hands of a few.

Truth is accessible to all. Truth simply is.

It merely exists.

Right, wrong or indifferent.

Truth is unchanged by opinion, facts, belief systems and coercion.

Truth remains unadulterated by observation. A tree is a tree is a tree.

The same tree can be made into wood for building or become home to a squirrel.

Either way the tree is still the tree.

I'm not making excuses here.

I just have thought for so long that God has never been given enough credit. I mean, religious consciousness in so many various fundamental institutions and separate fundamental religions have demoted him (of course, male, right?) to a glorified Santa Claus.

When, in fact, religions preach how God is an impenetrable mystery we cannot know anything about. When of course, the religious leaders, themselves, are in direct personal communication, fairly regularly, over their cup of coffee.

A bit contradictory isn't it? Follow me here.

God/Santa, keeps a list of everything children do right and wrong, then rewards all of them in a single night. He comes personally to each and every house to give children their Christmas presents.

God/Santa has his 12 disciples, (oops that is Jesus and Jesus is just all right by me!) I mean reindeer, and if kids are bad don't they get onions and a switch?

Furthermore, don't we give God/Santa cookies? That is what the offering plate is, isn't it?

I mean if we are righteous we go to heaven. Right?

If we are evil we go to hell. Right?

The mandates are made by religions, likened unto parents, discerning good and bad.

I did, indeed, dedicate this little book to my German Shepard, Marley, but even when you spell God backwards, it is still not particularly appealing.

I just don't think we have gotten any of this right.

I believe it to be so mysterious, the mystery itself, is incapable of solving its own mystery.

It is the only concept that works for me.

I believe many fundamentally religious institutions are based on false truths, demeaning and giving unjust due to the true God. In addition, they proclaim they are heavenly right, and each of the others are hellishly wrong.

They all may well be in many ways, utterly wrong. How right were they when they got themselves started? Each of them proclaiming direct inspiration from God.

The world isn't flat anymore. Am I correct?

It could in fact be older than 6,000 years. Am I correct?

The Sun doesn't revolve around the earth anymore. Am I correct?

I'm not getting on a soapbox here.

Just checking your pulse.

Have you ever considered, actually, who God may be? I have.

Here, is my conclusion.

Mysteriously undertaking the consciousness of God, my observation shows God cannot avail itself unto its own consciousness because that alone would make unavailable another the right to theirs.

Knowing gives way to a source in pursuit of a place to inhabit as does desire.

In my opinion, God cannot will.

God cannot demand.

That which is less than God can do both.

God cannot create life, for if God was to create life, God would then become responsible for Death.

Life and Death are responsible to each other.

The animation of Life. The animation of Death.

Although both are intensely real. A lion killing a gazelle.

There are only two ingredients to reality. All reality.

There is, All That Exists, and there is, All That Exists Not.

These two and only ingredients cannot be each other simultaneously.

God can only be, All That Exists Not.

All That Exists Not makes possible the manifestation of All That Exists.

God cannot create in God's own image, yet that which is not God, can do so easily.

An acorn tree all by itself can assuredly prove my point. One cannot know God.

Knowledge carries consciousness where even musing interacts with existence, and imbued into the shadow is a reflection that exists, which knows not whence, where, what, or how it:

Became.

The reflection that is mirrored is not the existence of the maker, of that reflection.

The closer one gets to God is a distance that can never be traveled.

A distance which cannot be, for if God were to become: God must then endure.

God must then sustain.

God would need another for the perpetuation of its own survival.

No longer would there be, all which is not, to give unto all that is to become.

All life exists, begins, ends and can never remain the same.

An existence that can never change is an existence that can never become.

That Which Exists Not, exists eternally to be evoked by That Which Exists, to sustain itself temporarily.

There can be nothing more able.

All That Exists exists because of, yet not inside of, All That Exists Not.

There can be nothing more able than that which has made possible, all things possible, yet, having no possibility itself.

There can be no greater sacrifice. There can be no greater ability.

There can be no greater love.

Availing to life, that which life cannot exist without, to be evoked upon by life, for its own self-existence.

For one to know, one must become.

If one were to know, that which knows not, one must become that which cannot be.

That which knows not can never be known.

When a particle of that which knows not, is evoked

into existence by that which exists, the particle can easily be known.

What can never be known, is that which knows not. That Which Exists Not.

Yet from the unknowing, accesses all knowing and partakes of nothing, and withholds selfish intent from consciousness, that yearns for something, and for something more.

While nothing infringes not, always remaining nothing unto another, making possible for all to become something.

Something will always be dependent upon something to remain existing unto itself.

Something will always be dependent upon something to perpetuate its own survival.

How could this be God?

Something will always require nothing to make material its initial manifestation, its Original First Cause.

Nothing never requires anything, and neither is nothing dependent upon something to remain in an existence of, That Which Exists Not, eternally, never changing, yet giving life to all.

In the beginning was the word and the word was God?

This could never be, because for the

word to survive, the word would need something outside of its own existence and wouldn't God be greater than that?

The word would need to multiply to survive; the word would be dependent upon the creation of God, which is Man, in God's own image.

This makes God nothing more than the beasts in the field.

The grasses on the high plains.

This makes God in need of survival.

Life itself is temporal, instinctual, endlessly chasing its own survival.

Life is born to die. God cannot be life.

Life lives in ultimate fear of Death.

Life survives unto itself, clings unto itself, takes and feeds upon another to insure unto itself more of itself.

Life creates Death, its greatest fear, for its own survival. God cannot be this.

That Which Exists Not, needs nothing to remain in its nonexistence.

Consciousness is dependent upon, That Which Exists Not, to bring itself into manifestation and yet will ultimately selfdestruct within its own self-existence.

Consciousness, returning back to the womb of nothing, only to become something more.

That Which Exists Not, has easily remained throughout the Aeons before time, throughout the Aeons of time and will easily remain when the Aeons of time will never be.

Yet That Which Exists Not, has existed in the essence of all because, All That Exists, partakes of the essence of nonexistence to make itself manifest.

Consciousness changes endlessly, in its pursuit of self-identity, in its illusion of eternity, weighing experiences of its reality, attempting to make itself more.

Consciousness, whether it to be bird, tree, human, Sun, Moon, Star Systems, more, much more.

The man-made consciousness of whatever God thinks is God, is its own perceived existence. Having been

Being manifest by its own self-interest, having been evoked from nonexistence, which can only be, God of All.

Meanwhile...there are only two choices:

That Which Exists, changes.

That Which Exists Not, changes not. So which one is God?

... and so the eternal now presents itself and in between our memories the hopes for a new tomorrow lie the field of all possibility.

For spring, undaunted, without a care for the frozen nights of winter beckons within her womb the stirrings of new life and the yearning to flower the beauty, she knows, and so too, does love, undaunted by yesterday's chill and the tentacles of ice that leave a heart barren, without the whispers of another, "I love you."

I know we are all guilty, having fallen from bridges of our own making. Gasping oxygen as the whole of us plunged far below life's murky waters.

We knew then, even then, when we knew each other that we would proudly walk alongside the devil and equally proud, hang alongside Christ on the cross.

I don't know why it is that we knew that, but we have been right.

Not only to those around us was an unreachable place of mystery, but within ourselves, held the same.

I don't know that we are better for it. I only know that it has become us.

We have always had within us the eternal flame of life, although, our bodies have been often beckoned to return to the spiritually organic matter that birthed us.

We have lived our existence within a paradox of opposites. Placing ourselves unabashedly in each other's eye has been our fierceness, for our own privacy.

Although our wings have grown as that of an angel. We still dine with the devil.

As collective consciousness, we have always known the equality of the black and the white.

We have been witnessed to much phenomena. We have made the blind see and have removed the crutch from the cripple.

We go into the darkness because we must, for the transformation of light.

I personally believed Christ when he said; "That which I do, ye shall do greater."

But I have paid a price.

My greatest mistake was turning too much water into wine.

But even now a new day dawns and nature herself stirs within the seedlings, where in autumn they fell from their place of refuge, and found themselves, abandoned in the deep foliage, that even the tree itself uses for its own nourishment.

But sprout they will.

www.ingramcontent.com/pod-product-compliance
Lightning Source LLC
Chambersburg PA
CBHW071726090426
42738CB00009B/1893